www.aislin.com

During Jean Chrétien's 12-day tour of the Middle East, one gaffe followed another

IN YOUR FACE

...and other recent cartoons by Aislin

With an introduction by Dalton Camp

Text by Terry Mosher

Book design and colourization by Mary Hughson-Mosher

McArthur & Company

Toronto

Other books by Aislin:
Aislin–100 Caricatures (1971)
Hockey Night in Moscow (1972, with Jack Ludwig)
Aislin–150 Caricatures (1973)
The Great Hockey Thaw (1974, with Jack Ludwig)
'Ello, Morgentaler? Aislin–150 Caricatures (1975)
O.K. Everybody Take a Valium!
   Aislin–150 Caricatures (1977)
L'Humour d'Aislin (1977)
The Retarded Giant (1977, with Bill Mann)
The Hecklers: A History of Canadian Political Cartooning
   (1979, with Peter Desbarats)
The Year The Expos Almost Won the Pennant
   (1979, with Brodie Snyder)
Did the Earth Move? Aislin–180 Caricatures (1980)
The Year The Expos Finally Won Something
   (1981, with Brodie Snyder)
The First Great Canadian Trivia Quiz
   (1981, with Brodie Snyder)
Stretchmarks (1982)
The Anglo Guide to Survival in Quebec
   (1983, with various Montreal writers)
Tootle: A Children's Story (1984, with Johan Sarrazin)
Where's the Trough? (1985)

Old Whores (1987)
What's the Big Deal? Questions and Answers on Free Trade
   (1988, with Rick Salutin)
The Lawn Jockey (1989)
Parcel of Rogues (1990, with Maude Barlow)
Barbed Lyres, Canadian Venomous Verse
   (1990, with Margaret Atwood and other Canadian poets)
Drawing Bones–15 Years of Cartooning Brian Mulroney
   (1991)
Put Up & Shut Up! The 90s so far in Cartoons
   (1994, with Hubie Bauch)
Oh, Canadians! Hysterically Historical Rhymes
   (1996, with Gordon Snell)
One Oar in the Water: The Nasty 90s continued in cartoons
   (1997)
Oh, No! More Canadians! Hysterically Historical Rhymes
   (1998, with Gordon Snell)
2000 Reasons to Hate the Millennium
   (1999, with Josh Freed and other contributors)
The Big Wind-Up! The final book of Nasty 90s cartoons
   (1999)
Yes! Even More Canadians! Hysterically Historical Rhymes
   (2000, with Gordon Snell)
The Oh, Canadians Omnibus (2001, with Gordon Snell)

Published in Canada by McArthur & Company, 2001 322 King Street West, Suite 402, Toronto, ON, M5V 1J2

National Library of Canada Cataloguing in Publication Data

Aislin
      In your face: and other recent cartoons

ISBN 1-55278-241-7

Canada—Politics and government —1993. —Caricatures and cartoons. 2. Canadian wit and humor, Pictorial. I. Title.

NC1449.A37A4 2001   971.064'8'0207   C2001-901664-6

Cover illustration by AISLIN
Layout, Design and Electronic Imaging by Mary Hughson-Mosher
Printed and Bound in Canada by Transcontinental Printing, Inc.

The publisher would like to acknowledge the financial support of the Government of Canada through the Book Publishing Industry Development Program (BPIDP) and the Canada Council for our publishing activities. The publisher further wishes to acknowledge the financial support of the Ontario Arts Council for our publishing program.

10 9 8 7 6 5 4 3 2 1

CONTENTS

INTRODUCTION

So, I'm in Montreal staying at the Ritz and calling around.

Almost all my Montreal friends are cosmopolitan anglo, like Nancy Southam. She was having a little drop-in party, cocktails and cheese and beer, so I took a cab and walked upstairs to a noisy room of strangers and full of body-heat. It was one of those period two-story houses on another of those endless Montreal streets that are like rivers, rising in the east end and falling on the bureaucracies outside Ottawa.

After finding a drink, I circled the room, like people do, searching for a face I might put a first name to. The search was unsuccessful and, you know how it is, I can't even find the hostess. A stranger, clutching a glass, emerges from the crowd and begins to chat me up. Not a big talker, but a man who can start a conversation without too much trouble. I guessed he knew who I was but was not impressed. Still, people who hang out at Southam parties are not usually missing persons and this guy, I figured, was famous for something, maybe in the insurance business.

So I said, perkily, "Sorry, I didn't get your name."

He looked at me, briefly. I could tell I had given myself away. Everyone would know him except a dumb Toronto Tory klutz like me.

"Terry Mosher," he said.

I remember he was badly dressed, just the way famously sophisticated people present themselves, letting you know they don't give a damn what you think of the unmade bed they're wearing.

I had never heard of Terry Mosher. As far as I was concerned, Terry Mosher was a total loss in my frozen, all black radar screen. If he had said he was Clark Gable I would have been pleased to meet him and would have enquired as to how Scarlet O'Hara was making out. But Terry Mosher?

I then proceeded to do what every ego-inflated, overly fool-hardy dumbstruck male would unerringly do. I made matters worse.

"Umm. Aaah. What do you do for a living, Terry?"

"I draw a little," he said.

The fates then rushed to my rescue, and about time. A smiling young woman interrupted the silence that had fallen between me and Mosher. "Hi, honey," she said, kissing him. "I didn't know you were here. How nice!" She took him away with her. I suspect he encouraged it.

Later, much, much later, I asked Southam about her friend. "Who was the guy who told me he draws?"

"That was Aislin," she said. "Everybody knows him."

"No," I argued. "He was a short sort of unhappy guy. Said his name was Mosher."

"That was Aislin!," she said, shouting. "Migawd! You didn't know Aislin? He's only a genius, that's all."

I bear no resentment. Of course I knew Aislin. Who doesn't? But he's not easy to know, if you're from Toronto and you don't know Aislin is really Terry Mosher's daughter, and any damnfool would know that. Of course he would. In closing, I might say I don't know Aislin, never had the pleasure of meeting her. And I really didn't get to know Mosher until he arrived in New Brunswick during the summer of 2000 in the company of Mary, who draws. The Moshers were touring my province and stayed awhile at Jim Ross's world renowned Clam Shack.

Since then it has been a golden year for cartoonists and no one has had more fun than Aislin. I had always thought that Duncan Macpherson had peaked during the Diefenbaker years: Duncan and Dief were made for each other and their partnership stood for years to rank as the cartoon canon of the generation.

But then came Stockwell Day who lightened the life and challenged the wits of a serious man like the gentle Terry Mosher. Great men, I have always believed, are born to rise to great occasions and grasp the nettle of opportunity. Aislin did for Stock what Duncan did for the Chief. I shall always remember the rain of insight and artistry, and the lunatic zest of the truly inspired. A compassionate friend who knows of my deep affection for politics would dispatch Aislin's inspirations to me by fax, bells ringing, wheels grinding, and the laughter of the gods echoing over the falling tides along the Fundy shore.

It was a hell of a great year. If it were a wine, it would have become one of the great vintages of our time. Once I found out who Terry Mosher really was, I ordered myself champagne.

Next summer, I hope to meet Aislin.

Dalton Camp
Fredericton, N.B.
July, 2001

OTTAWA

Talk about a cartoon-op...

In that most memorable visual moment of his short, meteoric career on the national stage, Stockwell Day had emerged from British Columbia's Lake Okanagan after his by-election victory, riding a Jet Ski and wearing a wet suit, to meet the nation's media.

That was in September, 2000, a few short months after Day had been nominated as leader of the newly-named Canadian Alliance party. If it had been Day's intention to present a radically different image to the public than that of the old political gas-bags that had reigned for so long in Ottawa, he succeeded – if however briefly.

In contrast, Prime Minister Jean Chrétien's game is golf; and his motto could very well be the same as the Holiday Inn slogan: "No surprises." He and his Liberals muddle along in their

AND THE LATEST GIZMO TO REDUCE POLLUTION? THE SLOW-FLO GAS NOZZLE...FOR POLITICIANS

DRIP →
← DRIP

ruling of this immense, diverse, sparsely populated country, the only political party to operate comfortably in Canada's two official languages.

In the process, Chrétien likes to keep things simple, surrounding himself with capable people who sort out the tricky bits for him. None is more efficient than his Finance Minister, Paul Martin, whose elimination of the deficit has resulted in now-massive surpluses, leaving the reigning Liberals with a delightful dilemma: What to do with all that extra cash flowing through their veins?

Because of this, Chrétien has had to lessen his usual demands of total fealty in

Some deep contemplation is required over several proposals on the future of Canadian public broadcasting

Finance Minister Paul Martin underestimates the size of the surplus again

Paul Martin's case. For the cameras, Martin presents the image of the faithful lieutenant, a sort of Paulie Walnuts of The Sopranos, if you will. In reality, the two men are very wary of each other. The Finance Minister begs his own respect and loyalty, having quietly built his own alliances which now divides the Ottawa Liberals into two very distinct camps.

Mind you, as Paul Martin awaits his turn, Jean Chrétien has sent out signals indicating his own ideas on who his successor should be. Briefly, he seemed to be grooming Jane Stewart, the daughter of his old pal, former Ontario Liberal leader Robert Nixon. After serving effectively as the Indian Affairs Minister, Stewart advanced to become Human Resources Minister in August of 1999.

However, within several months, Stewart seemed in over her head in a major "boondoggle," a word whose meaning had to be explained to the Prime Minister by a reporter from the National Post. Chrétien eventually was forced to come to Stewart's aid after a scandal broke regarding $1 billion worth of job-creation grants. For several months, the then-Reform Party in its most effective performance to date, and still under the tutelage of Preston Manning, hounded Stewart with damning questions in the House of Commons. Stewart's public persona was tarnished so badly that she eventually hired herself an image consultant.

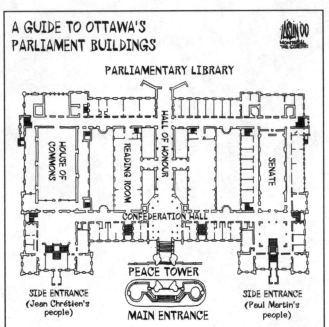

A GUIDE TO OTTAWA'S PARLIAMENT BUILDINGS

PARLIAMENTARY LIBRARY

HOUSE OF COMMONS

READING ROOM

HALL OF HONOUR

SENATE

CONFEDERATION HALL

PEACE TOWER

SIDE ENTRANCE (Jean Chrétien's people)

MAIN ENTRANCE

SIDE ENTRANCE (Paul Martin's people)

This was followed by Jean Chrétien's disastrous 12-day tour of the Middle East in the spring of 2000 whichwas riddled with an unheard of number of gaffes on the part of the PM. ("I don't know if I am in West, South, North or East Jerusalem.") After three years into their second term in power, the turning of the millennium seemed a time when the wheels could very well have begun falling off the Liberal machine.

Jane Stewart's performance in the Commons over bungled government grants leaves much to be desired…

...leading to the hiring of an image consultant

boon·dog·gle \'bün-ˌdä-gəl, -ˌdȯ-\ n [coined by Robert H. Link †1957 Am. scoutmaster] (1929) 1 : a braided cord worn by Boy Scouts as a neckerchief slide, hatband, or ornament 2 : a wasteful or impractical project or activity often involving graft — **boondoggle** vi — **boon·dog·gler** \-g(ə-)lər\ n

Canadian frustrations with Jean Chrétien were symbolically expressed with his being hit in the face with a cream pie by an aspiring playwright during a visit by the PM to a summer festival in PEI. If only Canada's growing number of opposition parties had been so effective. Instead, they were all having trouble getting their ducks in a row, overwhelmed by their own petty concerns.

"The Bloc Québécois was born to die," claimed Lucien Bouchard at the party's founding convention in 1990, trusting that its eventual demise would go hand in hand with Quebec's departure from Canada. Well, it's proving to be a slow death – and not in the manner originally intended. From a high point as the official opposition under Bouchard in 1993, the fortunes of the Bloc Québécois have continued to decline under the stewardship of Gilles Duceppe. Parochialism would seem to be the order of the day. One recent memorable headline regarding the Bloc involved their internal paradoxical squabble over whether or not to distribute free Canadian flags and lapel pins to their constituents.

On the left, the NDP has split into two factions: Those who wish to embrace a social democratic market-oriented platform in the style of Tony Blair versus the traditional union based left.

PM pied in PEI

15

"WHO KNEW?"

ITEM: BLOC WILL CONTINUE TO MAKE USE OF CANADIAN FLAGS...

Free Canadian flags are available to Bloc constituents

The NDP's process of trying to reinvent itself has resulted in most Canadians losing interest. By way of illustration, in the 2000 Federal election 38% of left-wing Canadians voted for the NDP, while 42% backed the Liberals.

The NDP also seems uncomfortable in charging the barricades in solidarity with the young growing international pro-democracy movement. The most attention that the NDP got out of the Summit of the Americas in Quebec City was Svend Robinson threatening to sue over his $300 slacks being ruined by police, supposedly by a plastic bullet. $300 slacks? Some socialist.

New Democratic MP urges radical overhaul of party

THIS, SIR, IS A DEAD PARROT!

McDonough's

ITEM: NDP LOOKS AT NAME CHANGE TO MAKE ITSELF MORE PALATABLE TO THE PUBLIC....

SOME FRIES WITH THAT?

The NDP holds a policy meeting in Montreal on the same weekend as the film Pearl Harbor opens

Plastic bullet ruined my pants at Quebec summit, NDP MP says

PLANS TO FILE COMPLAINT

BY JUSTINE HUNTER

OTTAWA • Svend Robinson, the New Democratic Party MP, vowed to lodge a complaint against the RCMP after a pair of his pants were destroyed during a protest at the Summit of the Americas in Quebec City.

Waving a plastic bullet and a spent canister of tear gas fired by police during the protest, Mr. Robinson told a news conference on Parliament Hill yesterday: "I lost a pair of pants and I have a wound on my leg."

Mr. Robinson said he was dressed in black casual slacks

SAY, IS THAT A PLASTIC BULLET IN THAT GUY'S PANTS? OR IS HE JUST REAL GLAD TO SEE ME?

AISLIN 01
MONTREAL
GAZETTE

Canada's new Governor General Adrienne Clarkson and her partner, author John Ralston Saul

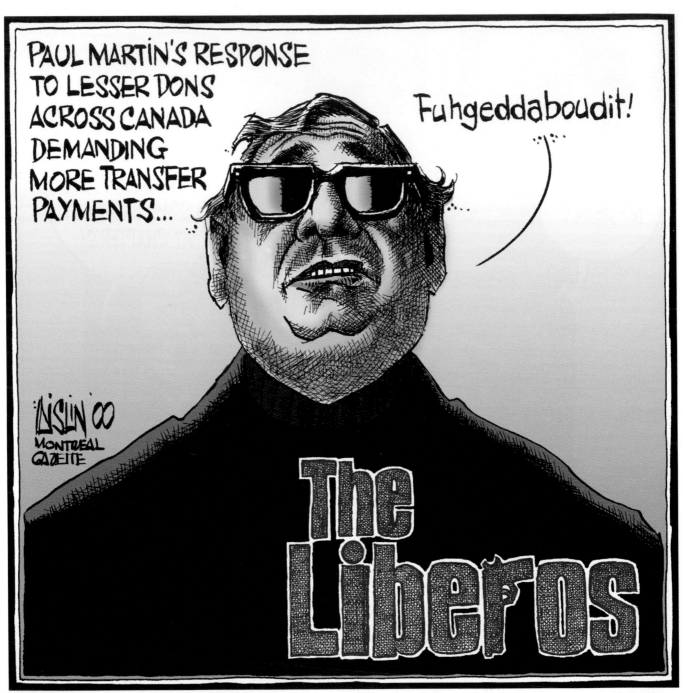

Is Paul Martin Canada's very own Paulie Walnuts?

Joe Clark's daughter Catherine seemed to be everywhere with him leading up to the 2000 election

A suggested new logo for the Canadian Alliance party

Preston Manning's Reform Party is frustrated in its attempts at becoming a national presence

Ontario's Tom Long

By 1999, Preston Manning, the Leader of the Opposition, realized that there was only one way to expand the Reform Party's support enough to elect him Prime Minister of Canada. He had to unite the right by somehow attracting the remnants of what remained of the Progressive Conservative Party, then floundering under their recycled leader, Joe Clark. Ordinarily a crafty politician, Manning put a plan into play that didn't take into account one crucial element: the fickleness of his own grass roots supporters. After a contrived process of eliminating the Reform Party's name by creating a new political party called The Canadian Alliance, Manning

Alberta's Stockwell Day

Joe Clark's dog

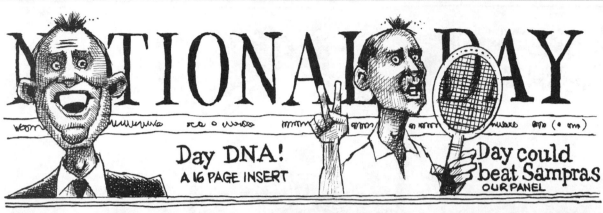

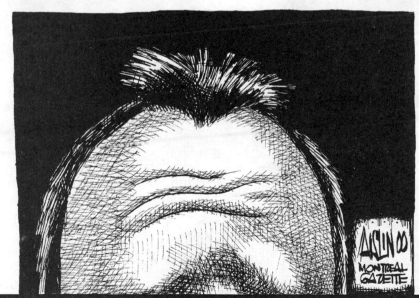

The right-wing National Post is positively euphoric over Stockwell Day

25

Stockwell Day confesses to having inhaled as a youth. But, did he ever exhale?

then called for a leadership review that was to backfire on him.

Two credible candidates stepped forward to challenge Manning gaining immediate national attention: Tom Long from Ontario, and Ralph Klein's Finance Minister in Alberta, Stockwell Day.

Long proved too much a product of Bay Street, raising traditional Canadian hackles. He was also singularly unilingual in comparison to Stockwell Day, who had picked up some French as a young man living in Montreal. Many in the media, particularly the two national newspapers, were intrigued with Stockwell Day's youthful image and antics. Day appeared to be a breath of fresh air compared to the stodgy Preston Manning.

Suddenly, Canada had a new karate-chopping leader of the opposition, where upon the Tories sank to single digits in the polls. Still, Joe Clark persevered, appearing wherever they would have him across the country, often with his attractive, politically-savvy daughter Catherine in tow.

Briefly, the Liberals appeared to be nervous about Stockwell Day, but then decided to take the offensive.

On the pretext of determining how Canadians wanted their government to spend the surplus, Jean Chrétien called an election for November 27, 2000, Canada's third in seven years. With Stockwell Day barely able to find his own way around Ottawa, the race was on.

There was immense curiosity across the land about this new youthful leader of the Canadian Alliance espousing family values. But with such scrutiny, cracks in his facade

Jean Chrétien calls an election

began appearing immediately. Within three days of the start of the election campaign, his Jet Ski began to sink. Appearing in crucial southern Ontario, Day likened the drain of young people to the U.S. to Niagara Falls flowing south. Informed that Niagara flows north, a sartled Day said: "We will check the record."

The Alliance launched a $63-million TV ad campaign focusing only on Stockwell Day, portraying him chopping wood and such.

Jean Chrétien played it low key by standing on the Liberal record during the crucial televised leadership debates, leaving it to Stockwell Day to create the only memorable visual moment, and an unfortunate one at that. The ground rules had forbidden the use of props. Nevertheless, Day twice held up a

And yet Joe Clark persevered

hand-scribbled placard reading: "NO 2-TIER HEALTHCARE, drawing the amused comment from Joe Clark that the Alliance leader was running for office, "as some sort of game-show host."

Chrétien triumphantly led the Liberals to re-election with an increased majority. The Alliance also increased their seat count but with hardly any crucial gains in the east.

On the Quebec front, Chrétien's Liberals caught up to the Bloc Québécois in both popular vote and seats. Conservatives and the New Democrats only managed to hold onto official party status.

By letting Stockwell Day hang himself, Jean Chrétien, who ten years earlier had been dismissed as yesterday's man, was now being hailed by the talking heads as a political genius.

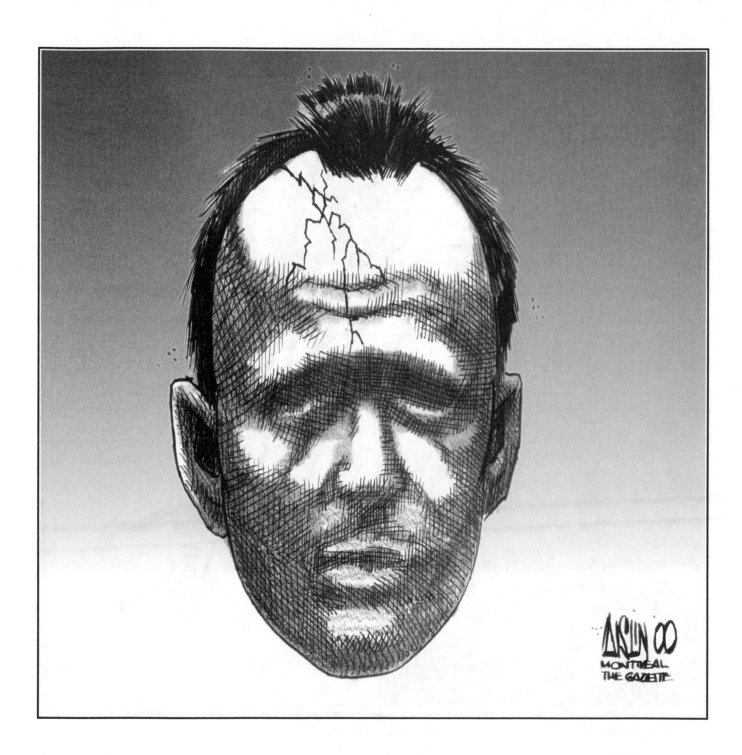

31

Alliance leader, Stockwell Day, gets the flow of Ontario's Niagara Falls wrong

Canadian Alliance television ad campaign focuses on a vigorous and athletic Stockwell Day

A game-show host?

Chrétien joins the ranks of John A. Macdonald, Wilfrid Laurier and Mackenzie King in serving three terms in a row

The national media descend on Burnt Church

NEW BRUNSWICK

In 1999, the Francophonie Summit was held in Moncton, ironically named after Robert Monckton who supervised Acadian expulsions in the 1700s. And then the Burnt Church lobstering crisis gained New Brunswick more national attention. With the local cartoonists down there having a field day, I decided to take a closer look. This New Brunswick sketchbook is a result, and the first in a series from different parts of Canada that will appear in future cartoon collections.

New Brunswick is called the drive-through province with travellers barreling through on their way to PEI or Nova Scotia. Having been guilty in the past of the same, I decided to spend ten days circling the province. It's a 6-CD drive from Montreal down to Madawaskan lumber country, Canada's most bilingual region. Overall, few seem to have a chip on their shoulder over language issues in New Brunswick...

Occurring 10 years after Oka, the Burnt Church native lobstering crisis has the potential for yet another ugly conflict

Federal fisheries officials under minister Herb Dhaliwal increase the pressure on Micmac lobsterers

A New Brunswick sketchbook...

IN CAMPBELLTON, N.B., WE FOUND A SCULPTURE OF "THE WORLD'S LARGEST FISH."

NEAR BATHURST, THERE IS "THE WORLD'S LARGEST STRAWBERRY."

SHEDIAC N.B.? "THE WORLD'S LARGEST LOBSTER."

NACKAWIC, N.B. IS THE HOME OF "THE WORLD'S LARGEST AXE."

...AND, IN HARTLAND WE DROVE OVER "THE WORLD'S LARGEST COVERED BRIDGE."

AND SO, WE CAME AWAY FROM NEW BRUNSWICK, BRIMMING OVER WITH IDEAS ON HOW THAT WONDERFUL CORNER OF THE WORLD MIGHT CREATE EVEN MORE SUPERLATIVE SITES...

MONCTON CLAIMS TO BE "THE FAST FOOD CAPITAL OF NORTH AMERICA. WHY NOT BUILD THE WORLD'S LARGEST DOUGHNUT?

FLORENCEVILLE IS HOME TO McCAIN'S. HOW ABOUT THE WORLD'S LARGEST SERIOUSLY TWISTED FRY?

TIDAL BORE

McCain HEAD OFFICE

"THERE'S NO SHORE LIKE THE NORTH SHORE—THAT'S FOR SURE!" ACTOR MARSHALL BUTTON as LUCIEN

FIDDLEHEADS
LOBSTER
CLAMS
FRESH SALMON
684-4142

JAMES WARD · BURNT CHURCH

ACADIEN TIRE

THE LIGHTHOUSE AT MISCOU, WHERE THE WINDOW FACING THE OCEAN HAS A WINDSHIELD WIPER.

PIZZA

Tim Hortons
ALWAYS FRESH
DRIVE THRU
BEST COFFEE & GOSSIP IN TOWN!

THE AVERAGE CANADIAN WILL USE 400 TREES IN HIS OR HER LIFETIME — ABOUT FOUR TRUCKLOADS OF LUMBER

MIRAMICHI'S FLAT IRON BUILDING IS CLASSIFIED AS A HISTORICAL SITE, DOUBLING AS A PIZZERIA

SAINT-FRANÇOIS-DE-MADAWASKA, N.B.

FOR THE BENEFIT OF TWO VISITORS, DALTON CAMP DOES DULCE!

Actually, it's a Crème Brulée

JACK AND JILL — ST. LEONARD, N.B.

In English-speaking areas of New Brunswick, signage is generally in English. Where French is spoken, signs are mostly in French. In between, everything is bilingual. How stunningly logical!

We continued along the north shore, enjoying the vista of the Gaspé across the Bay of Chaleur, to Acadian country where we stopped in at Burnt Church to see James Ward, the main Micmac provocateur. Media-savvy and cell-phoned, James nevertheless seemed not sure what to do with a cartoonist.

North of Miramichi is an ecological centre created by the powerful Irving family. Having made their fortune out of oil, pulp and paper, the centre seems an effort to make up for past sins.

Hurrying through popular Shediac region, we regained the road-less-travelled in the south-east region of Tantramar which, with it's wildlife areas, is one of

"MEANWHILE, AN OUTSIDE, EXPERT NEGOTIATOR HAS BEEN NAMED IN THE NEW BRUNSWICK LOBSTERMEN'S DISPUTE!"

Canada's best-kept secrets. We then went to the Petitcodiac River in Moncton to watch the aptly named three-inch, tidal bore. Locals claim that it used to come in at five or six feet. Sure. With expanding cultural activities, Moncton is the engine that will eventually drive the Maritimes' economy. There's some resentment about this down the road in Saint John which was once the financial capital of the Maritimes.

Continuing up the historical Saint John River valley, we were in for a final eccentric treat. In St. Leonard, we came across a pick-up truck with a beer-drinking couple sitting in back, covered in red and yellow slime. For a few dollars, friends were allowed to squirt mustard and ketchup on the engaged couple, helping to pay for their upcoming wedding. Called a "Jack and Jill" this ritual might explain perhaps the plunging marriage rate in the Madawaska region.

Back to business as usual in the House of Commons

OTTAWA

"This guy here is the leader of the Opposition! This guy!"

Deborah Grey pointing at Stockwell Day
in the House of Commons

After the Federal election in November of 2000, Ottawa got back to the same old same-old, with the Liberals as arrogant as ever with their increased majority.

However, controversy was mounting over Shawinigate, with legitimate questions being asked about Jean Chrétien's involvement in the ownership of a hotel and a golf course in his home riding. The confusing details on the matter stretched well back over a decade.

Nevertheless, the Alliance Party, up until now so adroit in the House of Commons as the official opposition, fumbled the ball badly on this one. With parliament's resumption, it became apparent that the neophyte Stockwell Day had some difficulty working with other members of

Liberal largesse continues on the home front

PM volunteers questionable documents on Shawinigate

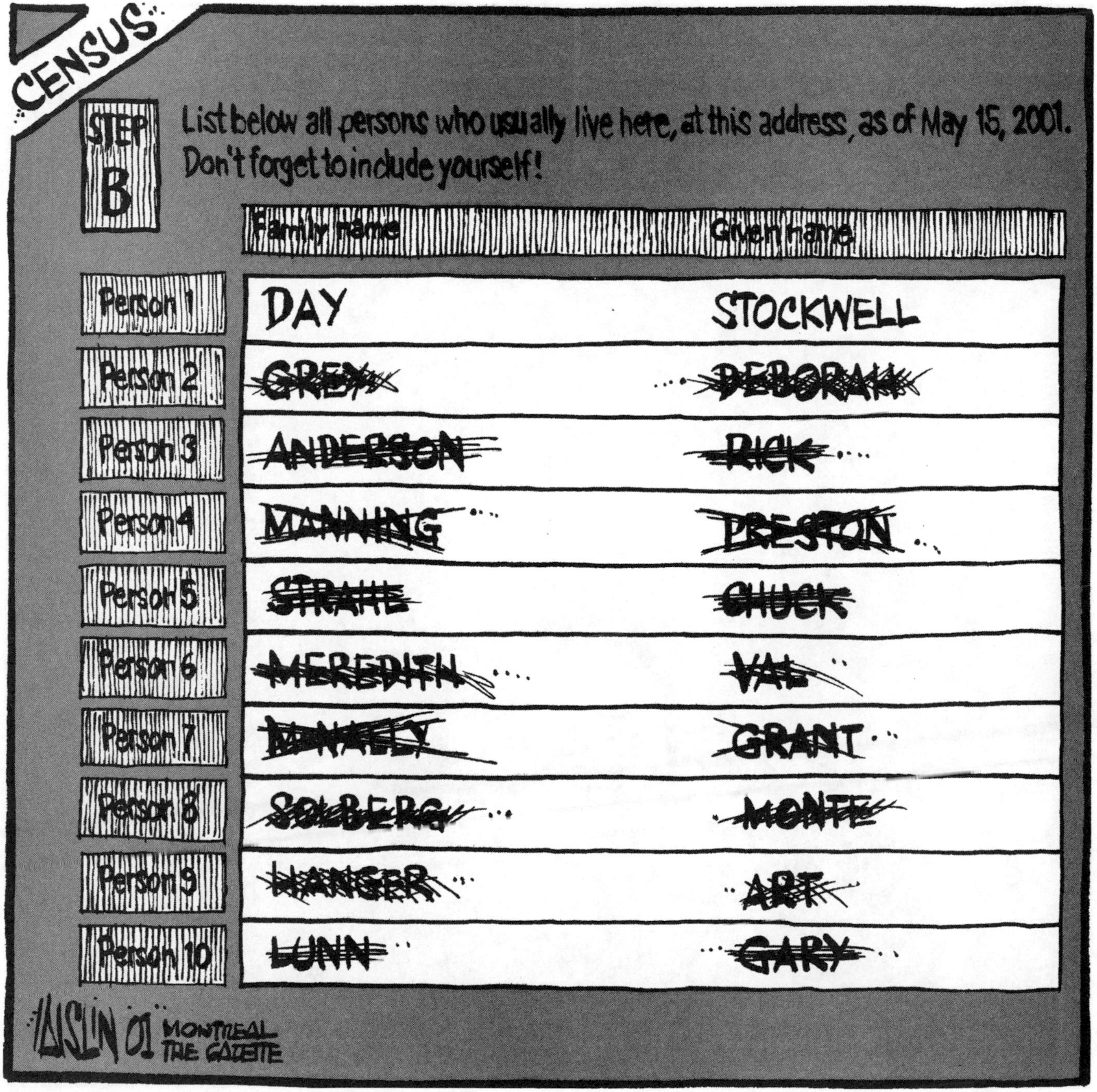

AS THE FLOODING SEASON BEGINS...

Spring, 2001

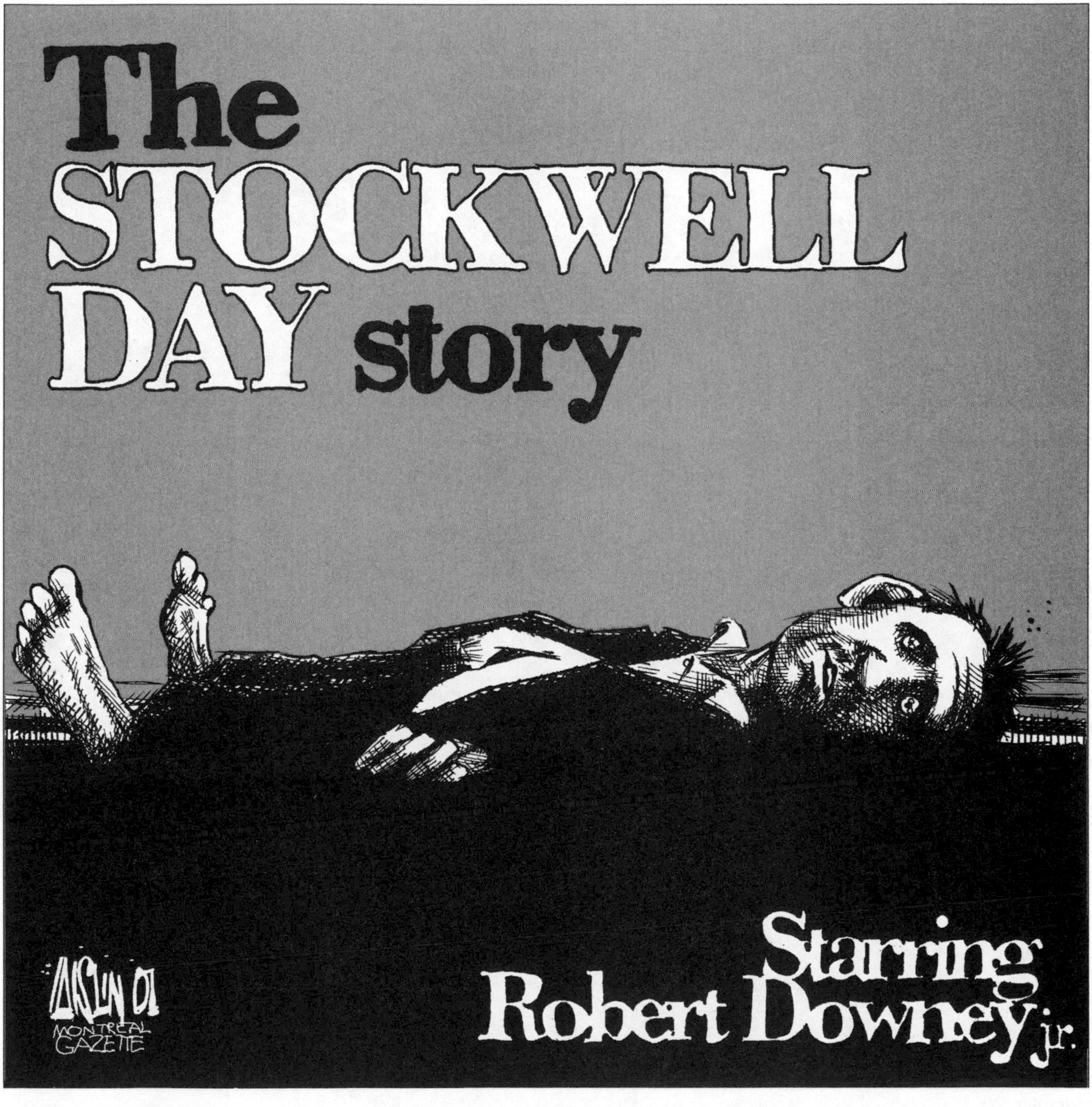
The
STOCKWELL
DAY story
Starring
Robert Downey jr.
AISLIN 01
MONTREAL GAZETTE

Summer, 2001

COMING THIS FALL!

Canadian Alliance leadership race

Much anticipation about the release of the film The Lord of the Rings in the fall of 2001

Federal ethics counselor, who was appointed by Jean Chrétien, clears the PM

his team. Day bungled badly on an $800,000 defamation lawsuit that had been brought against him by an Alberta lawyer, alienating his former boss Ralph Klein. Even more attention was deflected from the Alliance's performance in Parliament with them hiring a private investigator to get information on the Liberals. Other problems kept cropping up for the hapless Stockwell. With the rapid descent of the Alliance in the polls, Day began fleeing his own press conferences and, by the spring of 2001, members of his own party began quitting on him with demands from all fronts for his resignation.

PM visibly upset by Joe Clark's questions in the House of Commons

By the summer of 2001, the polls had the Alliance at 6%. The fortunes of Stockwell Day in were in free-fall, contrasting sharply with his spectacular ascent the previous summer.

Meanwhile, it was Joe Clark who emerged from the electoral ashes to pick up the torch and lead the charge against Jean Chrétien and Shawinigate. Immediately after the election, the federal ethics counselor, Howard Wilson had cleared Chrétien in the matter. The R.C.M.P. followed suit, saying that there was no basis for an investigation. Nonetheless, the experienced parliamentarian Clark continued to pit-bull Shawinigate in the House of Commons, much to Jean Chrétien's chagrin as the PM began ducking Joe's questions.

Lo and behold, by the summer of 2001, the Tories were close to 20% in the polls with Joe Clark's personal popularity skyrocketing up the charts. Joe Clark, smiling broadly, was suddenly everywhere: Quebec's Fête nationale, a

gay pride parade, and the Calgary Stampede, jauntily dressed in cowboy hat and bolo, all the while flipping flapjacks. Daily now, Clark was being quoted in the nation's press with ongoing speculation that he might be the only person around capable of uniting the right and leading it again out of the wilderness.

None of this appeared to worry the governing Liberals for the moment. With the closing of Parliament in the spring of 2001, the Liberals passed an unheard of gigantic pay and pension increase for all federal parliamentarians.

"...ALL DA' WAY TO DA' BANK!"

ASLIN 01
MONTREAL
THE GAZETTE

Prime Minister gives himself a 40% pay raise

Of more immediate concern and speculation amongst Liberal watchers in Ottawa was the matter of how long Jean Chrétien planned on remaining at the helm.

Who will eventually replace Jean Chrétien?

Former Prime Minister Brian Mulroney starts speaking out publicly on a number of issues

Jean-François Lisée releases his book Sortie de Secours (translation: Emergency Exit) that speculates on the future of Quebec

Louise Beaudoin wants to save France itself from the dreaded encroachment of the English language

QUÉBEC

"The language issue is not what it used to be."
Josée Legault, The Gazette

It was another Louise Beaudoin moment, her going ballistic about the "imperialism" of the English language. "I think it is scandalous. Scandalous!" she barked, but this time against Air France for forcing air-traffic controllers in Paris to communicate in English. She was absolutely right, but it didn't stop me from drawing the cartoon on the left of Louise barrelling into Charles de Gaulle Airport. Whenever Louise had anything to say about language, it was now expected that I do a cartoon on the matter.

However, after five years serving as the minister in charge of language, Beaudoin was relieved of her duties, moving on to International Affairs and ending my run of caricaturing her as a whip-wielding dominatrix.

Merci, Louise. All good things must end.

Jean Chrétien introduces his Clarity Bill, clearly aimed at future Quebec referendums

Shaken by the closeness of Quebec's referendum five years earlier, and determined to never have the country ever go through a similar exercise again, Jean Chrétien closed the millennium with the introduction of his draft bill on clarity. The brain child of Intergovernmental Affairs Minister Stephane Dion, the bill was clearly aimed at Quebec and meant to clarify Ottawa's role in case of any Quebec attempt to secede from Canada.

The clarity bill, upon close inspection, is anything but. In the words of Gazette columnist, Don MacPherson, "The draft bill contains weasel words that leave Ottawa plenty of the kind of wiggle room that politicians like, and in some pretty important areas."

Out of Quebec came predictable grumblings about the bill and its authors, Chrétien and Dion, neither of whom are popular in their home province. Some attempts were made by Lucien Bouchard to beat the drum on this, hoping to jump-start emotions in favour of "winning conditions" for another referendum.

However, the Quebec public just weren't interested, perhaps preoccupied with their own problems at home. In the midst of hospitals experiencing crises in emergency rooms, it was discovered that Health Minister Pauline Marois was busy redecorating her office to the tune of

OUR MASTER OF CLARITY...

IN ANSWER TO *VOTRE* QUESTION, LET ME MAKE IT CLEAR THAT IF THEIR QUESTION ISN'T CLEAR LIKE WE THINK OF AS BEING CLEAR WELL, FOR SURE, WE WILL CLEARLY NOT HAVE ANYTHING TO DO WITH THAT THERE UNCLEAR QUESTION ...NEXT QUESTION?

IS STÉPHANE DION'S STRATEGY WORKING?

JEAN CHRÉTIEN THINKS SO... AFTER ALL, HE'S NO LONGER THE MOST HATED MAN IN QUÉBEC

Should the life-sized statue of René Lévesque have a pedestal?

PQ stalwart makes untoward comments about Jews

With hospital emergency rooms in crisis, Quebec health minister Marois redecorates her office

WITH QUEBEC EMERGENCY ROOMS IN CRISIS, BERNIE LANDRY CHECKS OUT ANGLO-SAXON INTEREST RATES IN TORONTO...

Finance minister Landry parks federal grants slated for health care in a Toronto bank to gain interest

Former premier Jacques Parizeau continues to publicly pass comment on Lucien Bouchard's way of doing things

Bouchard resigns

$400,000, including a silent-fill toilet and an Imperial corner shower. Then it was disclosed that Finance Minister Bernard Landry had parked an $841-million federal health care transfer payment in a Toronto bank to gain a little more interest.

Bill Clinton came to Mont Tremblant and gave a speech in favour of "a strong and united Canada," while a Quebec Court Judge in Granby struck down a crucial section of the provincial language law.

Was it any wonder then that Lucien Bouchard, who was never trusted by the hard-liners as was made evident in speeches by former premier Jacques Parizeau, appeared to be losing interest?

When separatist hard-liner Yves Michaud made some untoward remarks about Jews, Lucien Bouchard, probably under domestic pressure to get out of the game, stepped down to sign up with a

A BIG SHOE TO FILL...

AISLIN '01
MONTREAL
THE GAZETTE

prestigious Montreal law firm. Indeed, Bouchard's departure was so complete that, several months later, he couldn't be bothered to attend the Bloc Québécois' 10th anniversary party.

The PQ party faithful had cooled on Bouchard as much as he had on them. To replace him, they turned to their reigning stalwart, Bernard Landry, who had proved himself capable over the years serving under various regimes. But Landry also had a history of opening his mouth a little too wide at times, with no one knowing what might tumble out. Landry found himself in hot water while complaining about the number of visible Canadian flags in Quebec, comparing them to "red rags." He was forced to backtrack, insisting his meaning was lost in translation. And then, shortly after that, Landry, on a visit to a clown school, claimed that Quebec was desperately in need of more clowns!

AND SO, AS THE PQ LEADERSHIP RACE BOILS DOWN TO A FIGHT BETWEEN TWO MEN—BERNARD LANDRY (THE CRAFTY OLD POL) AND BERNARD LANDRY (THE VILLAGE IDIOT)...

Bernard Landry says that Quebec has a need for more clowns

In Canada's largest ever security operation, 6,000 police officers protected Quebec City during the Summit of the Americas

75

A wire fence was constructed around the centre of Quebec City to keep out the 30,000 protesters

Soon, noises were being made about Landry being given more recognition at the Summit of the Americas, which was to be held in Quebec City in April of 2001. Thirty-four heads of state, along with 9,000 FTAA delegates, were invited, protected by 6,000 police officers carrying out the largest Canadian security operation ever.

Journalists were kept busy covering the coalition of 30,000 protesters beyond the 4-kilometer-long security fence.

For inner-city locals, most of whom are dependent on the tourist trade, the Summit proved to be one gigantic dud with much of the traditional tourist activity curtailed. Most hid out at home, waiting for the tear gas to clear and the circus to get out of town.

Next time, suggested one Quebec City wag, a far more suitable location for a similar summit might be someplace like the West Edmonton Mall.

Not the Quebec City we know and love

The famous Quebec City caleches are not allowed to operate during the Summit

With the Summit of the Americas over, residents get to reclaim their city

Bonhomme Carnival as Summit mascot?

Bernard Landry calls the Canadian flag a red rag

BUSINESS

Could representative politics as we had intended them simply disappear in the 21st century? Yearly, politicians seem increasingly redundant as their roles become more that of water-carriers for the people who really run things: all these CEOs who seem intent on making the world into one massive corporation. And haven't they found their man now in George W. Bush – a.k.a. Dubya – a person most thought of initially as the dimmest bulb in the lamp?

Mind you back in November of 2000, the final decision on who would be the next President of the United States – George Bush Jr. or Al Gore – couldn't be determined for over a month because of questionable voting practices in Florida and some highly suspect tabulation methods. We sat riveted watching CNN, learning at least that a chad is not necessarily a country in Africa.

Six days out of seven, Canadian political cartoonists will draw on Canadian subject matter for inspiration. That's our job and

it's expected of us. Besides, who else in the world cares or pays attention to Canada? On those days when little is happening at home, we'll venture into

Oldsmobile to be discontinued by General Motors

Will General Pinochet ever go to trial to face human rights charges?

SHALOM...

Hard-liner Ariel Sharon is elected Prime Minister of Israel

89

China is granted the Olympic Games for the summer of 2008

ITEM: THE EMBARRASSINGLY PROFITABLE ROYAL BANK WILL TRIM 1,500 JOBS

Heh, heh. WELL, WHAT WITH 2 OR 3 VICE-PRESIDENTS AROUND HERE DEMANDING BONUSES...

international territory, passing comment on Russia, say, or the deplorable conflict in the Middle East.

However, with business edging politics off the front page, the world of finance is more of a target for satirists, and will contine to be for as long as we are allowed to do so – not too much longer, I suspect.

TAX CUTS...

Universal call from big business for tax cuts

REPORT ON BUSINESS

Former RT Capital player is seeking new opportunities...

RT Capital Management stock manipulation exposed

For a period of time, dot-com stocks rock…

...and then come tumbling back to earth

SAY, WE'RE HAVING SOME DIFFICULTY
CONNECTING WITH THESE WEB SITES:
www.askjanestewart.ca
www.investincinar.com
www.martymcsorleyfanzine.com
www.ndp.ca
www.fillerup.com
www.johnmccain2000.com
www.joeclarkforpm.ca
www.minoritiesforgeorgewbush.com
www.jeancharestspeaksup.ca
www.pinochetcrazylikeafox.com
www.séparation.qc

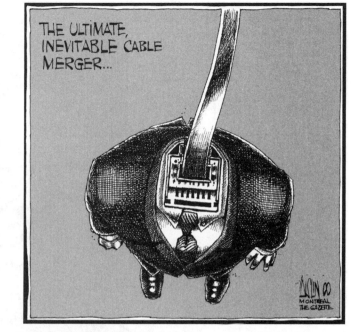

THE ULTIMATE,
INEVITABLE CABLE
MERGER...

YOU'VE GOT MAIL!!!

From	To	Subject
Jean Chrétien	Paul Martin	ILOVEYOU
Joe Clark	The National Post	ILOVEYOU
Conrad Black	Jean Chrétien	ILOVEYOU
Preston Manning	Tom Long	ILOVEYOU
CBC	CRTC	ILOVEYOU
Pamela Wallin	Peter Mansbridge	ILOVEYOU
Joe	USA	ILOVEYOU
Céline Dion	Shania Twain	ILOVEYOU
William Johnson	Jean Charest	ILOVEYOU
Bernard Landry	The Gazette	ILOVEYOU
Guy Bertrand	Serge Chapleau	ILOVEYOU
La Presse	Jeffrey Loria	ILOVEYOU
Jeffrey Loria	Jean Coutu	ILOVEYOU
Expo fans	Rob Braide	ILOVEYOU
Peter Trent	Louise Beaudoin	ILOVEYOU
Louise Beaudoin	Terry Mosher	ILOVEYOU

JEEZ, HOW BIG CAN THESE MERGERS GET?

AND THIS JUST IN.
MOMENTS AGO, God.com
ANNOUNCED THE MERGER
OF CHRISTIANITY, ISLAM
AND JUDAISM...
THERE IS NO INDICATION
SO FAR THAT THE MOVE
WAS A HOSTILE ONE

I LOVE YOU virus hits computers world-wide

The size and scope of business mergers intensify

Conrad Black sells off most of his newspapers in Canada

Canadian government is forced to backtrack on information gathering

In a major police sweep, 135 bikers are arrested in Quebec

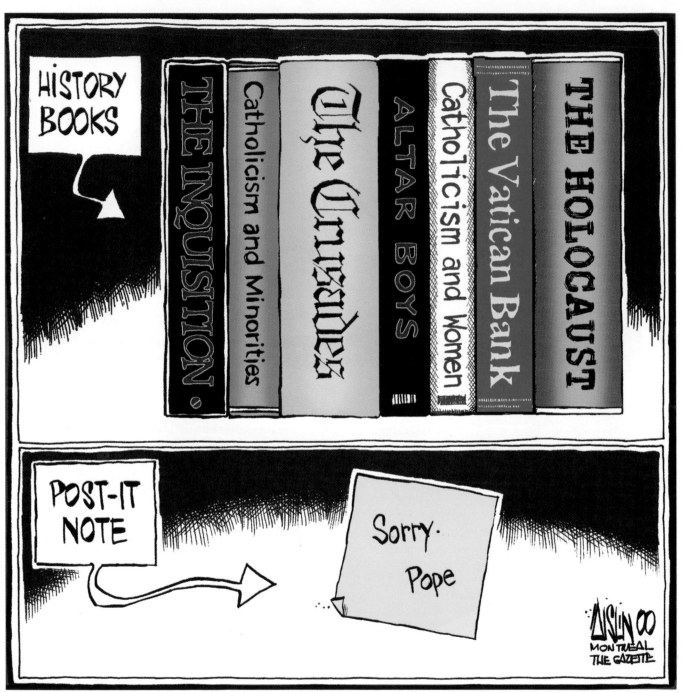

The Pope issues a brief apology for the Church's past indiscretions

Money's going out of style

Use of debit cards in Canada is overtaking cash

KAREN HOWLETT
Financial Services Reporter, To...

D ebit cards are for th...
running neck and ...
cash as Canadians'
method of payment ...
overtake it.

A recent survey s...
year, 38 per cent o...
said they chose debit ...
withdraw money direct...
bank accounts, as ...
method of payme...
time, the survey ...
Association said ...
respon...
old-fa...
Chequ...
per c...

views with 2,157 Canadians in February.

THE NEW Panhandler?

...e said. "So the popularity of
...stic starts...rly.
...upscale M...swear chain Harry
...most customers use their
...ds for big-ticket purchases
...he "smallest percentage"
...store manager said.
...t-card trend is even
...g when compared with
...ago.

on page A8

ASLIN '00
MONTREAL
THE GAZETTE

LIFE

"Life. Consider the alternative." Whomever

Well, yes, there is that, isn't there? Still, we resent so many ominous forces that come into play while we negotiate the complicated daily business of life, all the while trying to make a buck. So many unfathomable elements now mock our bedrock concepts of justice, democracy and fairness: the arrogance of big business, globalization, our children's Pokémon cards. Who understands the rule book anymore especially when there doesn't appear to be one?

No wonder we're nostalgic for simpler times. Take crime. We understood it. We'd all seen Godfathers I, II and III, right? But now, the bikers have taken over from the traditional Mafia in certain key areas like the sex trade, drugs and gambling.

Oops, sorry. It was the government that co-opted gambling now, wasn't it?

Singer Ginette Reno performs at Hells Angels wedding

Montreal crime reporter Michel Auger shot by an assailant

21% of players are pathological gamblers

Video Lottery Terminal...

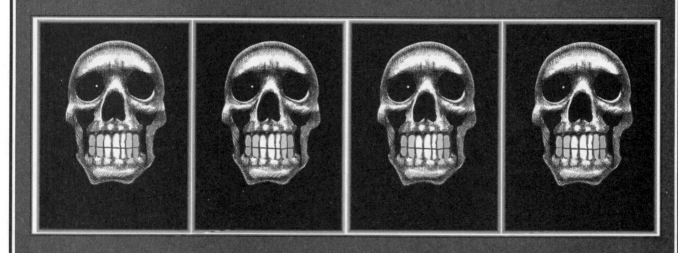

Over a two year period, 48 suicides in Quebec are attributed to gambling

NEWS ITEM: AIR CATTLEPROD ADDS 2,000 JOBS!

107

Frankly, this is the first time as a Dermatologist that a teenager has asked me how to *get* acne...

And what about the confounding business of trying to get from Point A to Point B? Airline companies now treat us as if we had mad-cow disease while prodding us from one airport holding pen to another, resulting in an escalation of air-rage occurrences within the herd.

Speaking of transportation, automobile manufacturers have now cajoled a majority of car owners into believing that they actually need a truck instead – a monster, gas-guzzling, four-wheel-drive SUV – to get to the mall. All the while, we talk incessantly on cell phones that, if science can get it right, may soon be imbedded into our small, receptive brains.

Our kids have adopted ragged fashions and pallid tastes that makes them look like teenagers on chemo.

We tentatively passed into the new millennium, legitimately concerned about the ever-increasing extremes in global weather, caused essentially by our own over-consumption. Will the Kyoto Protocol on emissions ever be actually honoured by the international community? Will we ever find a cure for the common cold? Will the Red Sox ever win the World Series?

The answer, my friend, is blowin' in the wind – and Bob Dylan is sixty.

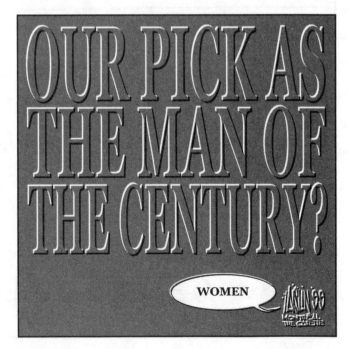

February is usually Montreal's harshest month

Meanwhile, a Gazette survey selects Montreal's best submarine sandwich reataurants in the middle of a July heat wave

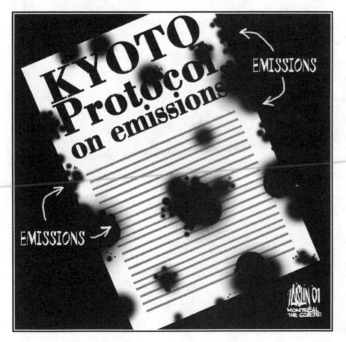

On an up note, more books, such as the Harry Potter series, are now being sold than ever before. However, in Canada the industry verged on collapse because of the mismanagement of the mega-bookstore chain Chapters.

Free trade negotiations between Canada and the United States brought out an interesting contrast: what we call culture, the Americans call entertainment.

No problem. We sent them some – Pamela Anderson's breasts and Céline Dion's Vegas act! Here at home, left all alone with culture, we were preoccupied with our own usual concerns. The CBC continued brutal cutbacks to local news programming outside of Toronto. The national broadcaster is now seriously considering getting more into sports – and changing its call letters to TBC.

And, why not?

Toronto regards itself as the centre of culture for all of Canada. The city celebrated this by erecting several hundred hand-painted life-sized moose sculptures in the streets. The idea had been suggested by the CEO of McDonald's Restaurants of Canada who stole the idea from Chicago, which had done the same thing with cows several years earlier.

But then, Toronto is a world-class city.

Pamela Anderson's

113

Céline and René renew their vows in an extravagant ceremony in Las Vegas

In a grand public spectacle, Céline Dion's first-born is christened at Montreal's Notre Dame Basilica. A camel even showed up

This cartoon is a tribute to underpaid and under-appreciated school teachers everywhere

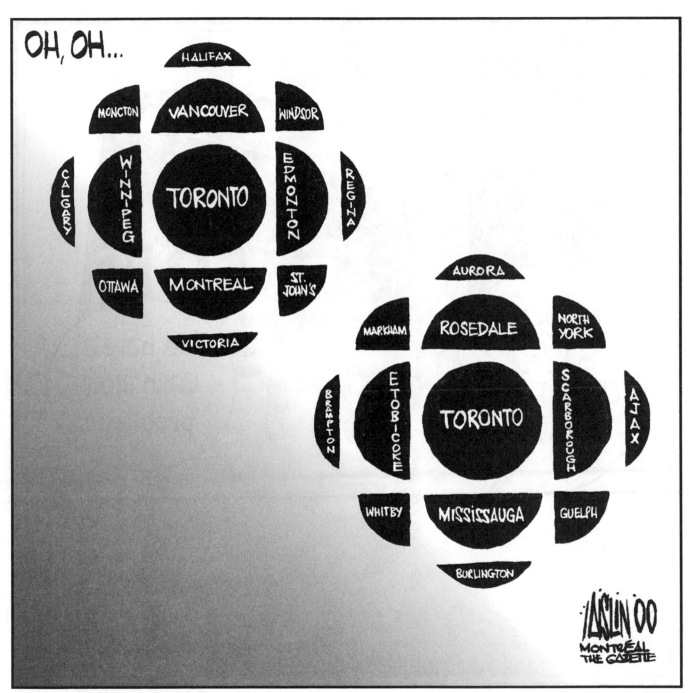

Ongoing CBC cutbacks in the boonies

The problems in the Canadian book publishing industry all lead back to Chapters

Margaret Atwood

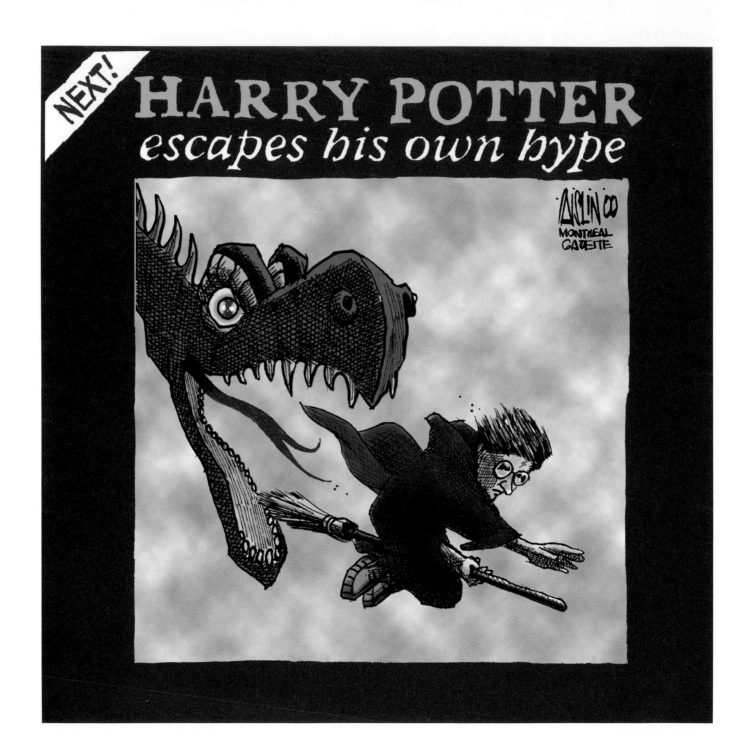

Spring training sketchbook of the projected opening day batting order of the Montreal Expos, Jupiter, Florida, 2001

It didn't take long for Montrealers to sour on New York art dealer Jeffrey Loria who had bought the Expos

SPORTS

The fortunes of the Montreal Expos continued to spiral downward through the late 1990s. With the baseball team under the direction of Claude Brochu and an oddball coalition of squabbling minority local owners, Montreal fans were hopeful that some strong individual might step forward – a Charles Bronfman type, say – to lead the team back from the road to oblivion. Well, Montrealers got far more than they had bargained for.

In 1999, Jeffrey Loria, a New York City art dealer and life-long baseball fan, bought a controlling interest in the Expos. The initial reaction was euphoric in Montreal, particularly after it was discovered that Loria even spoke some French. Optimism continued when several passable ball players were actually acquired for the 2000 season. And talk continued about construction of a user-friendly downtown baseball park to replace the ominous and distant Big O, the bane of Montrealers since its construction for the 1976 Olympics.

Would Jeffrey Loria be the saviour of baseball in Montreal?

However, suspicions began to emerge that the new owner might be working on his own agenda. Over the next eighteen months, Loria, to quote Gazette sports columnist Jack Todd, "...systematically alienated the limited partners, the fan base, their sponsors, the media and just about everyone else." Plans for the new stadium were suddenly put on a shelf and English-language broadcasts of Expos games, long a Montreal tradition under the popular Dave Van Horne, were lost to listeners for the 2000 season. Van Horne, perhaps seeing the writing on the wall, is now the play-by-play broadcaster for the Florida Marlins.

Popular Expo manager Felipe Alou's days appeared numbered on opening day, 2001

2,200 volunteers showed up to participate in a nude art happening in the streets of Montreal

Jeffrey Loria fires Expos manager Felipe Alou

In the spring of 2001, with attendance dwindling and the team performing below .500, Loria fired Expos manager Felipe Alou, the most popular baseball figure in the thirty-three year history of the club.

Montrealers' taste can turn on a dime. To quote another Gazette columnist, Pat Hickey: "The Expos are no longer considered cool." Most seem resigned to the idea that the baseball team may be lost to Virginia or Las Vegas. Besides, how could Montreal possibly keep up in an era when one baseball player was signed by the Texas Rangers to a quarter-of-a-billion dollar contract to play shortstop?

As a society, we give lip service to the idea that participation in sport is its own special reward. In reality, fame and endorsements come only to those who finish first.

On the world stage, the spectacular 2000 Summer Olympic Games held in Sydney, Australia, were plagued by eleven positive drug tests resulting in five athletes being stripped of medals. Denial seemed the order of the day with accused athletes playing the role of "victim," claiming they had no idea how banned substances might have arrived in their systems. C.J. Hunter, a former world-champion American shot-putter whose multiple positive tests had been covered up in the past, held a tearful press conference pleading his innocence accompanied by none other than lawyer Johnnie Cochran. These theatrics were dismissed by Montrealer Richard Pound, a vice-president of the IOC and chairman of the World Anti-Doping Agency, as "the usual excuse." The International Olympic Committee had come under some hard scrutiny itself after it was revealed that many members had been bribed in the awarding of the Olympic Winter Games to Salt Lake City. Several blatant abusers were then kicked out.

Much of the responsibility for the IOC's restructuring had fallen to Pound, who also negotiated multi-million dollar

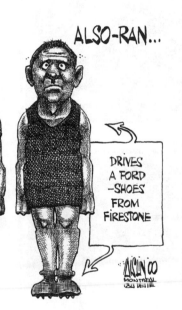

MEDAL WINNER...   ALSO-RAN...

MULTI-MILLION DOLLAR DEALS WITH MERCEDES AND NIKE

DRIVES A FORD —SHOES FROM FIRESTONE

AISLIN 00
MONTREAL
GAZETTE

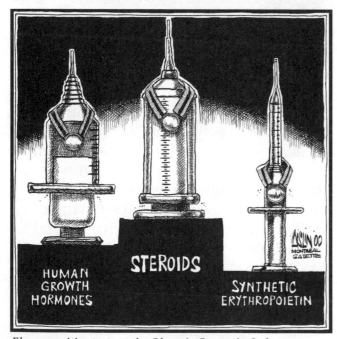

Eleven positive tests at the Olympic Games in Sydney

Richard Pound loses IOC presidency bid

After embarrassing remarks by mayor Mel Lastman, Toronto loses out to Beijing in its bid for the 2008 Olympic Games

Jacques Villeneuve is once again eliminated early at Montreal's Grand Prix

television deals for the IOC, saving the outfit from financial ruin. Yet, when IOC president Juan Antonio Samaranch stepped down, Pound, the most deserving candidate, was bypassed for the presidency, perhaps for knowing where too many skeletons were buried. Pound agreed to stay on as a member of the IOC although resigning all of his key posts.

At the meeting of the IOC in Moscow in the summer of 2001, Beijing was awarded the 2008 Olympic Games. Toronto, a contender in a bid for these same games, was embarrassed by remarks made by the city's mayor, Mel Lastman. When it was suggested that he woo delegates in Africa, the mayor made an unfortunate joke about not going to a place like Mombasa, where he saw himself being placed in a pot of boiling water surrounded by dancing natives.

Montreal's busiest weekend is in June when hundreds of thousands of racing fans descend on the city to see the annual Grand Prix on Circuit Gilles Villeneuve, named after the late Formula One racer. Gilles' son Jacques has moved on to even greater international fame, becoming the world champion in 1997. Next to Céline Dion, he is our most famous Montrealer, appearing in ads for Honda, his team's engine supplier. Plagued by a series of mechanical problems and mishaps over the last few years, Jacques was once again eliminated in Montreal's Grand Prix.

On a shoddier front, Montreal boxer Davey Hilton was charged with the sexual assault of two teenagers. At the trial, things were revealed that we really didn't need to know, like Hilton's occasional use of an elastic band during sex to retain a floating testicle.

Boxer Davey Hilton on trial for sexual assault

In the exciting Stanley Cup finals of 2001, the Colorado Avalanche – because of the astonishing performance of former Montreal goalie Patrick Roy – were finally victorious over the superior New Jersey Devils, who were coached by former star Hab defenceman Larry Robinson. These days, hockey-mad Montrealers have to search far and wide for a reason to keep their interest up, given that Les Canadiens haven't made the playoffs for three years running. Adding insult to injury, the much-improved Toronto Maple Leafs have recently advanced in the playoff rounds further than any other Canadian hockey team.

Even the Molson family, traditionally a strong supporter of sports franchises in Montreal, seemed to be throwing in the towel. When it was announced that the Habs were up for sale, initially there were no takers. George Gillett, an America meat packer, finally stepped forward, making himself a sweetheart deal in acquiring both a controlling interest in the hockey club and the newly constructed Molson Centre for a mere $275 million. Rumours then surfaced that, with the U.S. economy in a bit of a downturn, Gillett was actually quite short of cash. Finally, the deal could only be arranged through a local loan to the new owner from a consortium of Montreal credit institutions.

So there you have it: the Habs are owned by an American, George Gillett; the Expos by an American, Jeffrey Loria; and the Montreal Alouettes by an American, Robert Wetenhall.

With the death of cartoonist Charles Schulz, will Snoopy have to seek out endorsements?

The New Jersey Devils kept trying to find a way to beat Patrick Roy and the Colorado Avalanche in the Stanley Cup finals

Maple Leafs captain Mats Sundin

Montreal is out of the playoffs…again

The Molsons put Les Canadiens up for sale

Would an American buy the Habs?

The new American buyer of Montreal's hockey club appears to have cash flow problems

Globalization seems to be the hallmark of the new millennium, bringing with it an inevitable erosion of our sense of place in the 21st century.

How symbolic it seemed then when Maurice "The Rocket" Richard died on May 27, 2000. He was born in Montreal, had made his reputation internationally as a Montrealer, and died in Montreal.

I doubt we'll ever see his kind again.

"Hockey was bigger than the church, and the Rocket was bigger than the pope."

NHL Hall of Fame referee Red Storey

Maurice Richard dies

138

A FEW REASONS WHY I LOVE MONTREAL

Aislin

1-Church spires everywhere

2-Breakfast and the newspapers at l'Express on St. Denis

Cool..

3-Caging myself a ride on radio station **CJAD**'s traffic helicopter to see Mont Royal's wonderful foliage in the autumn

4-Blowing the budget and renting yourself a heated garage in the depths of February

GIOVANNI

ROTISSERIE Italienne

5-Discovering yet another terrific inexpensive restaurant, like the Rotisserie Italienne, loved by all the visiting hockey players

DICKIE MOORES

6-Dickie Moores

TRIVIA QUESTION: WHICH MONTREALER ONCE CLAIMED TO HAVING BEEN LAID ON TOP OF THE MILK BOTTLE?

7-The Guaranteed Milk bottle at the foot of Crescent Street

GUARANTEED PURE MILK CO

Answer: Nick Auf der Maur

WARNING: NORTH OF HERE IS LAVAL AND THEN THE NORTH POLE

Mountain

WARNING: GO THIS WAY TO REACH WESTMOUNT AND OSHAWA

WARNING: IN THIS DIRECTION LIES REPENTIGNY AND BELGIUM

3

2

AVENUE DES PINS

PARC

MAIN

ST. DENIS

11

SHERBROOKE

5

SAINTE-CATHERINE

ATWATER

GUY

PEEL

UNIVERSITY

7

RENÉ-LÉVESQUE

6

10

SAINT-ANTOINE

4

6

6

6

NOTRE-DAME

1

8

WELLINGTON

FYI: Bridge to Casino AKA: Idiot's Alley

River

12

9

12

12

12

12

WARNING: SOUTH OF HERE IS ONLY BROSSARD AND OBLIVION

8-Watching the tugboats at work in the Old Port

9-Just minutes by bike from downtown are ducks, blue herons and terns in the Domain de la Forêt on Nun's Island

10-People volunteering to serve up a meal at the Old Brewery Mission, the city's oldest and largest homeless shelter

11-July in Montreal: The Jazz Festival, the Comedy Festival, the Red Sox

JAZZ

WISELY, OUT OF TOWN

12-Getting out of town on the loud and overcrowded weekend of the Grand Prix

A map of Montreal drawn for the National Post

Canada goosed! My favourite cartoon of Mordecai Richler

MONTRÉAL

Montrealers have gathered too often of late in Place d'Armes, eyes turned towards Notre Dame Basilica, saying goodbye to their legends: Maurice Richard, Jean Drapeau and Pierre Trudeau. Mordecai Richler's funeral, a smaller affair at the request of his family, received similar national attention and emotional outpouring from his admirers.

These four individuals are remembered for diverse reasons and thought of in different ways, depending on people's political bent or what newspaper they might read. Nevertheless, no matter how disparate, all four of them were united in their Montrealness.

The passing of Pierre Trudeau, such a elegant, dashing and vigourous individual in private and public life, seemed to particularly bring us all up short, reflecting perhaps on our own mortality. There was the expected solemn dignity for a funeral of a former Prime Minister of Canada, but also a certain need-to-be-

Montreal mourns the death of Pierre Trudeau

there in the streets. Jimmy Carter, Leonard Cohen and Fidel Castro standing shoulder to shoulder as honorary pall bearers were, according to rumour, later spotted in Montreal's Intercontinental Hotel hoisting a toast to Trudeau.

"Migawd, only in Montreal!" observed our female witness to all this.

Justin Trudeau's moving televised eulogy to his father galvanized all observers, creating inevitable national speculation about the possibility of a political future for this – yes – charismatic young man: "Or perhaps the quieter brother Sacha?"... "And what about Ben Mulroney?"... "Or

The three wise men go to Ottawa

Declaring the War Measures Act

The morning after Quebec's 1980 referendum

Trudeau…or Thatcher?

Dancing with Stanfield

Trudeau returns after Joe Clark's brief stint as Prime Minister

P.E.T. resigns

Jean Drapeau dies

Mordecai Richler dies

'ELLO, MORGENTALER?

"THE OLYMPICS CAN NO MORE HAVE A DEFICIT THAN A MAN CAN HAVE A BABY."

JEAN DRAPEAU.

ASK NOT WHAT YOU CAN DO FOR YOUR COUNTRY, BUT RATHER, "WHAT CAN YOUR COUNTRY DO FOR YOU?"

"Mordecai Richler, who died last week, had by the end of his life become inseparable from a place, Montreal, and even a country, Canada, without ever flattering or even saying anything particularly nice about either. One of the gifts of Canadian life is that it is not necessary to be loving in order to be loved."

Adam Gopnik
The New Yorker
July 16, 2001

Mordecai Richler is buried on Mount Royal not far from his old drinking pal, Nick Auf der Maur

the politically savvy Catherine Clark for that matter?"…"And, while we're on the subject, how about all those Richler kids?"

There is some satisfaction at least in knowing that our best and brightest have indeed passed the torch.

Radio talk show host André Arthur has called Montreal the ultimate Canadian city, what with its traditional French and English history, and a rapidly growing population of newcomers who are now moving into positions of influence and power. It is no surprise that Montreal, more than any other city is pro-actively romanced by both federalist and separatist forces, both knowing that Montreal is the cotter pin on which their future aspirations turn.

Montrealers are very good at dancing the dance with both Ottawa, and Quebec City. However, as either Québécois or Canadians, most seem to think of their city as coming first, allowing a variety of people of different political persuasions to live and work very well together.

Leonard Cohen had expressed the wish back in the 1960s that Montreal become a separate city state. Delighting in its own eccentricities and ongoing street festivals, is it any wonder that the surveys always show Montreal to be the happiest city in Canada? Tourism is now Montreal's number one industry, in large part because of its many five star restaurants, and hundreds of excellent cheaper eateries serving up the world's cuisine.

The kids are okay

CAMPAIGN POSTERS, 2010?

JUSTIN Trudeau Liberal

VOTE CATHERINE CLARK CONSERVATIVE

BEN MULRONEY for the ALLIANCE

AND, FOR PRIME MINISTER IN 2030, SARAH COYNE?

AISLIN 00
MONTREAL GAZETTE

Pastrami vs. Smoked Meat

SPCA is burglarized

July Jazzfeast

Montreal's
International
Jazz Festival

Three Second Cup coffee shops in Montreal are firebombed for having an English name

Furthermore, business is picking up, despite narrow nationalism sometimes still rearing its ugly head. Rhéal Mathieu, a former FLQ member who had been imprisoned in the 1960s, was recently convicted for fire bombing several Second Cup coffee shops.

Overall, though, the city seems to be moving on, having recently experienced a mini-boom in downtown construction. More companies are now setting up shop, typified by the Ontario food giant Loblaws, now with a number of successful outlets in the Montreal region.

heavy-handedly – by the Quebec government under Municipal Affairs Minister Louise Harel and the current mayor of Montreal, Pierre Bourque. The reasons given for doing this have to do with historical municipal bickering and a need for fiscal equality on the Island of Montreal.

A majority of natives – in the suburbs anyway – are upset about this process, pointing out Toronto's financially disasterous amalgamation. Suspicion has also been expressed that this is an effort on the part of the PQ to erase English towns.

Louise Harel, the PQ's Montreal amalgamation dominatrix

On January 1, 2002, Montreal will become a mega-city composed of a number of subordinate boroughs replacing the 26 existing autonomous municipalities. Masterminded – often

The first city-wide municipal election will be held in November of 2000, with Pierre Bourque the present front-runner.

It could be lively. Stay tuned…

Montreal is experiencing a building boom for the first time since the 1970s

SLICES OF LIFE IN MONTREAL: Our roving sketchbook captures a Quebec nationalist, secretly shopping at Loblaw's....

Heh, heh...

Ontario's food giant Loblaws is proving to be very popular in Quebec

Oh, oh....

ONE CITY - One snowplow!

THE SINGLE, MOST COMPELLING, ARGUMENT AGAINST ONE ISLAND, ONE CITY?

OCCUPÉ

A MONTREAL CIVIL SERVANT

A PETITION, WORTH THE PAPER IT'S PRINTED ON....

1st PAGE OF THE PETITION IN FAVOUR OF ONE CITY...

Pierre Bourque	Nicole Lemieux
Andrée Gagnon	Guy Langevin
Serge Grenier	Marie Boucher
Vincent Leduc	Ginette Dubé
Jeanne Pelletier	Jean-Marie Roy
Gilles Lacroix	Yvan Tessier
Joseph Gendron	Paulette Noël
Jacques Morinier	Suzanne Poirier
Monique Bélanger	François Dorion
Manon Houle	André Michaud
Bernard Paquin	Pauline Monette
Francine Martin	Michel Vachon
Louis Rochon	Josée Trottier
Dominique Hébert	Maral Paradis
Alexandre Nadeau	Robert Marleau

HOLD ON...IT'S ALL IN THE SAME HANDWRITING!

Mayor Pierre Bourque comes up with a suspicious petition in favour of the amalgamation of Montreal

With amalgamation the charming little community of Montreal West will disappear

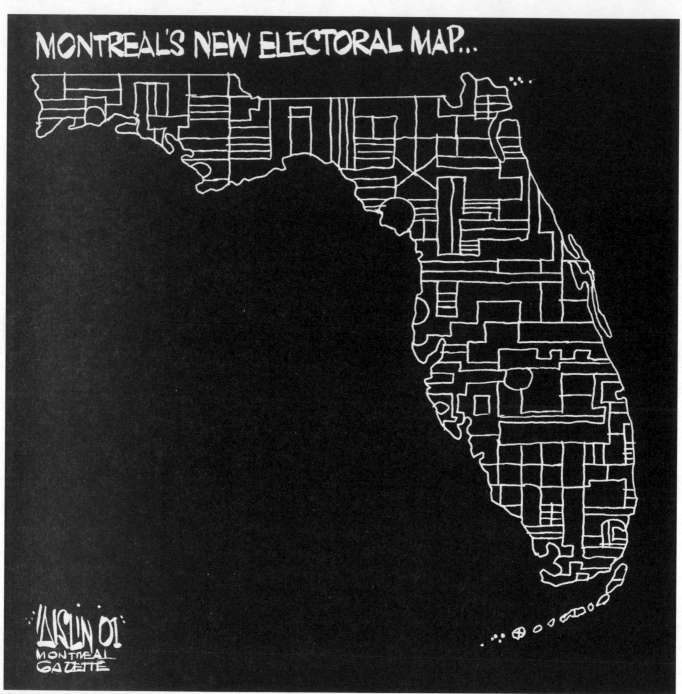

Bureaucrats present Montreal with an extremely confusing electoral map

AISLIN is the nom de plume that Terry Mosher has used for almost 30 years as the editorial page cartoonist for The Gazette in Montreal. Widely syndicated, Mosher has free-lanced internationally for The New York Times, Time Magazine, The National Lampoon, Harper's and Punch.

Aislin has travelled extensively, drawing for the Gazette from many corners of the world. Recently he has begun a series of sketchbooks on different Canadian provinces. The first on New Brunswick is included in this volume, while additional sketchbooks will appear in future Aislin collections.

Born in Ottawa in 1942, Mosher attended fourteen different schools in Montreal, Toronto and Quebec City, graduating from the École des Beaux-arts in 1967. He then began working for The Montreal Star, moving over to The Gazette in 1972.

The recipient of two National Newspaper Awards and five individual prizes from The International Salon of Caricature, in 1985 Mosher became the youngest person ever to be inducted into The Canadian News Hall of Fame. The launching of the home page featuring the daily Aislin Gazette cartoon on the Internet led to it being judged Canada's most entertaining web site.

Montreal's McCord Museum recently hosted a large exhibit of the best caricatures of Aislin and those of his confrere Serge Chapleau, the editorial page cartoonist for La Presse. The exhibition ran for 17 months and attracted 115,000 visitors.

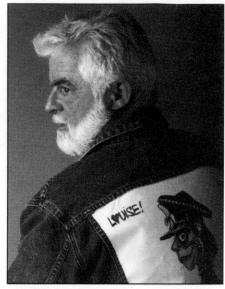

Photo: Cheryl Hnatiuk, The Gazette

An avid baseball fan, Mosher is a twenty-year member of The Baseball Writers' Association of America, which allows him to vote for Baseball's Hall of Fame in Cooperstown, N.Y. He is also a member of the board of directors of The Old Brewery Mission, Montreal's largest shelter for the homeless.

IN YOUR FACE is Aislin's 32nd book.

For additional information, including locations to order earlier books, please go to: **www.aislin.com**

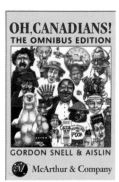

These recent Aislin collections are also available from **McArthur & Company**

Special thanks for help in the preparation of this volume go to:
Gaëtan Coté, Pat Duggan, Dave Stubbs, all those scary women at McArthur &Company, Stockwell Day for happening along and, most of all, Mary Hughson-Mosher